Women in Physics

Major Women in Science

MAJOR WOMEN IN SCIENCE

Women in Physics

Shaina Indovino

Mason Crest

Mason Crest
450 Parkway Drive, Suite D
Broomall, Pennsylvania 19008
www.masoncrest.com

Printed and bound in the United States of America.

First printing
9 8 7 6 5 4 3 2 1

Series ISBN: 978-1-4222-2923-1
ISBN: 978-1-4222-2930-9
ebook ISBN: 978-1-4222-8899-3

The Library of Congress has cataloged the
          hardcopy format(s) as follows:

          Library of Congress Cataloging-in-Publication Data

Indovino, Shaina Carmel.
  Women in physics / Shaina Indovino.
      pages cm. – (Major women in science)
  Audience: Grade 7 to 8.
  Includes bibliographical references and index.
    ISBN 978-1-4222-2930-9 (hardcover) – ISBN 978-1-4222-8899-3 (ebook) –
ISBN 978-1-4222-2923-1 (series)
  1. Women physicists–Biography–Juvenile literature. 2. Physics–Vocational guidance–Juvenile literature. I. Title.
  QC15.I53 2014
  530.092'52–dc23
                              2013011154

Produced by Vestal Creative Services.
www.vestalcreative.com

Contents

Introduction

Have you wondered about how the natural world works? Are you curious about how science could help sick people get better? Do you want to learn more about our planet and universe? Are you excited to use technology to learn and share ideas? Do you want to build something new?

Scientists, engineers, and doctors are among the many types of people who think deeply about science and nature, who often have new ideas on how to improve life in our world.

We live in a remarkable time in human history. The level of understanding and rate of progress in science and technology have never been greater. Major advances in these areas include the following:

- Computer scientists and engineers are building mobile and Internet technology to help people access and share information at incredible speeds.
- Biologists and chemists are creating medicines that can target and get rid of harmful cancer cells in the body.
- Engineers are guiding robots on Mars to explore the history of water on that planet.
- Physicists are using math and experiments to estimate the age of the universe to be greater than 13 billion years old.
- Scientists and engineers are building hybrid cars that can be better for our environment.

Scientists are interested in discovering and understanding key principles in nature, including biological, chemical, mathematical, and physical aspects of our world. Scientists observe, measure, and experiment in a systematic way in order to test and improve their understanding. Engineers focus on applying scientific knowledge and math to find creative solutions for technical problems and to develop real products for people to use. There are many types of engineering, including computer, electrical, mechanical, civil, chemical, and biomedical engineering. Some people have also found that studying science or engineering can help them succeed in other professions such as law, business, and medicine.

Both women and men can be successful in science and engineering. This book series highlights women leaders who have made significant contributions across many scientific fields, including chemistry, medicine, anthropology, engineering, and physics. Historically, women have faced barriers to training and building careers in science,

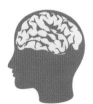

6

which makes some of these stories even more amazing. While not all barriers have been overcome, our society has made tremendous progress in educating and advancing women in science. Today, there are schools, organizations, and resources to enable women to pursue careers as scientists or engineers at the highest levels of achievement and leadership.

The goals of this series are to help you:

1. Learn about women scientists, engineers, doctors, and inventors who have made a major impact in science and our society
2. Understand different types of science and engineering
3. Explore science and math in school and real life

You can do a lot of things to learn more about science, math, and engineering. Explore topics in books or online, take a class at school, go to science camp, or do experiments at home. More important, talk to a real scientist! Call or e-mail your local college to find students and professors. They would love to meet with you. Ask your doctors about their education and training. Or you can check out these helpful resources:

- *Nova* has very cool videos about science, including profiles on real-life women scientists and engineers: www.pbs.org/wgbh/nova.
- *National Geographic* has excellent photos and stories to inspire people to care about the planet: science.nationalgeographic.com/science.
- Here are examples of online courses for students, of which many are free to use:
    1. Massachusetts Institute of Technology (MIT) OpenCourseWare highlights for high school: http://ocw.mit.edu/high-school
    2. Khan Academy tutorials and courses: www.khanacademy.org.
    3. Stanford University Online, featuring video courses and programs for middle and high school students: online.stanford.edu.

Other skills will become important as you get older. Build strong communication skills, such as asking questions and sharing your ideas in class. Ask for advice or help when needed from your teachers, mentors, tutors, or classmates. Be curious and resilient: learn from your successes and mistakes. The best scientists do.

Learning science and math is one of the most important things that you can do in school. Knowledge and experience in these areas will teach you how to think and how the world works and can provide you with many adventures and paths in life. I hope you will explore science—you could make a difference in this world.

Ann Lee-Karlon, PhD
President
Association for Women in Science
San Francisco, California

1

What Does It Take to Be a Physicist?

When you throw a ball across the room, how does it move? It might go straight across the room at first but then curve down. When it reaches a wall, it will bounce off. Eventually, it will stop moving and stand still. The laws of physics can explain every movement this ball makes. Physicists study these laws and try to figure out what causes them.

As the ball flies across the room, different forces are acting upon it. One force is gravity. Gravity is the invisible force that pulls all objects on Earth toward the center of the Earth. It is what keeps you on the ground and pulls you back down after you jump up. Another force is the one you are applying as you toss the ball. Finally, air resistance plays a role. Even though air might seem transparent or invisible, it is actually made up of tiny particles. Think of the way you swim through a pool. As you push your arms and legs, the water works against you. Air resistance is just like that except it is easier to move through than water.

Physicists understand all these forces. They study how objects move and why. The smallest of these objects are subatomic particles. These particles are the smallest unit known to humans, and they cannot be seen with the naked eye. The largest objects a physicist might study are planets, galaxies, or even the entire universe. In this way, physicists study everything that could ever possibly exist. Physicists are always trying to find out more about how the world works and why.

Physics can be applied to anything you do. Whether you are writing on a piece of paper, swimming in the ocean, or watching the moon in the sky, physics has allowed all these things to happen. As you go about your daily routine, pay special attention to what you do. Feel your feet push against the ground as you walk. Notice how the sun's rays seem to warm up your skin. Watch your chest rise and fall as you breathe in and out. All of this is caused by physics!

Many physicists become fascinated with the world when they are young. They continually ask questions. Why are there stars in the sky? What causes the Earth to revolve around the sun? How do birds and airplanes fly? Physics offers answers to all of these questions and more. And even with all of these answers, there are still so many discoveries to be made. To make matters even more confusing, some theories in physics conflict with other theories. They are so different, in fact, that they cannot both be true. There are many debates about how the physical world works. Above all else, physicists are always trying to explain to the world why it is the way it is.

Education

The best way to become a physicist is to start early. While you're in high school, do your best to take every physics-related class you can. This includes math classes, such as algebra and calculus. You will need to use complex formulas to understand how objects move.

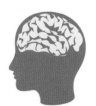

If you study physics, you'll be doing a lot of math. Physicists use mathematical equations to understand and prove how the physical world works.

Going to college is a necessity for physicists. As an undergraduate student, you may wish to pursue a general degree in physics. Choosing a **specialty** can be done later in graduate school. Earning a bachelor's degree usually takes about four years. Take extra courses in mathematics or engineering, which will help you later.

To become a **research physicist** or professor, you will need to earn a master's degree or PhD. Because the field is so vast, many physicists choose a specialty while pursuing advanced degrees. If you are interested in what causes the planets and galaxies to move, consider astrophysics. A person who cares most about subatomic particles might become a particle physicist. If you have already got-

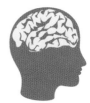

ten this far, you will probably already know which subfield of physics interests you the most.

Character

All physicists must be curious and open-minded. Curious people are more likely to look at something and wonder why it is the way it is. This "sense of wonder" has created some of the world's best physicists. The open-mindedness is needed to accept changing theories about our world. Just a few hundred years ago, many scientists were convinced that the universe revolved around the Earth. Today, we know better. We wouldn't have made this discovery if it weren't for open-minded scientists!

Physical science can be very complex and sometimes confusing. Trying to find a solution to a problem can be frustrating. Some physicists spend years on the same project before they finally have a breakthrough. A successful physicist will never stop looking for new possibilities. She needs to be patient and **persistent**.

Women physicists with all these qualities have made important breakthroughs in this field. Some of them even helped lay the foundations on which today's physicists build.

Words to Know

Specialty: a particular area of study requiring certain knowledge and skills.
Research physicist: a scientist who investigates the properties of matter and energy.
Persistent: unwilling to give up.

Find Out More

American Physical Society Sites, "Becoming a Physicist"
www.aps.org/careers/physicists

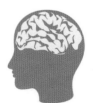

Education Portal, "Physicist Education Requirements and College Degree Information"
www.education-portal.com/physicist_education.html

Hollihan, Kerrie Logan. *Isaac Newton and Physics for Kids: His Life and Ideas with 21 Activities*. Chicago, Ill.: Chicago Review, 2009.

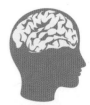

2

Lise Meitner:
Discovering
Nuclear Fission

For some of the earliest female physicists, obtaining a proper education was a real struggle. In Lise Meitner's day, women were not accepted and sometimes not even allowed in the sciences. This included physics. Although the odds were against her, Lise rose to the occasion. She became very successful as a female physicist. One of her greatest accomplishments was as part of a group that discovered nuclear fission. She was a physicist that worked with atoms.

Lise Meitner was born on November 7, 1878 in Vienna, Austria. She was exceptionally good at mathematics, and as a child, she was tutored in math. She was also interested in science. Education was very important to Lise's father. He believed that everyone should have an education. He insisted that his daughters receive the same education as his sons.

With the help of her parents, Lise achieved the education in science she craved. Physics became her specialty. In 1905, she earned a doctoral degree in physics from the University of Vienna. Lise was only the second woman to do so from such a large university. While in school, she met some important scientists who would later help her with her career. One of these was Max Planck.

After receiving her doctorate, Lise went to Berlin to learn even more. (Berlin is a large city in Germany.) She eventually became the assistant of Max Planck, who is best known for coming up with quantum theory. Quantum theory deals with physics on a microscopic level. Sometimes, quantum physics directly goes against the physics of larger objects. This can be confusing to physicists trying to find a link between the two. Until meeting Lise, Max Planck had rejected women in his lectures. After meeting her, he was convinced that women had **potential** to be great physicists.

A Woman of Many Talents

In addition to her knowledge in physics, Lise knew about medicine. She served as a nurse during World War I.

Throughout her career, Lise helped with several important discoveries. In 1917, while she was doing postdoctoral work, she made an important discovery with Otto Hahn, a chemist in Berlin.

All objects in the universe are made up of different atoms. Atoms are made up of protons, neutrons, and electrons. The number of protons an atom has determines what kind of atom it is. For example, an atom of carbon has six protons, while an atom of oxygen has eight. Each **element** can also have several isotopes, which are determined by the amount of neutrons an atom contains. Lise Meitner and Otto Hahn discovered many new isotopes together.

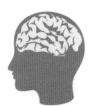

Lise with her mentor Otto Hahn, working in their laboratory in 1913.

At the same time, Lise became very interested in radiation. Certain elements are radioactive. As these elements decay, they release energy. This energy can be dangerous, but scientists have also found ways to use it to help people.

In 1926, Lise became the first woman to hold the position of full professor at a university. Then, in 1933, Hitler came to power; because Lise was a Jew, she was in danger. She fled Germany in 1938 and traveled to the Netherlands and Sweden, before settling down in Copenhagen, Denmark.

There she met with her old partner, Otto Hahn, and continued her research. She was part of a team that realized one element could be changed to another when a lot of nuclei were forced to collide with the original element. It was Lise Meitner and her nephew who realized this was nuclear fission.

Lise was asked to work on developing the atomic bomb, but she refused. When the atomic bomb was used in World War II, Lise did not approve.

Otto Hahn was awarded the 1944 Nobel Prize in Chemistry for his work in discovering nuclear fission. Many historians have argued that Lise Meitner deserved to receive the award as well because she was equally important in the discovery.

Lise Meitner died in 1968. She is remembered as one of the first successful female physicists. Her **resolve** and intelligence allowed her to excel in a world

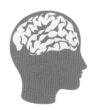

Nuclear Fission

Atoms are made up of subatomic particles. The nucleus is at the center of an atom, and it is made up of protons and neutrons. When a nucleus is broken apart, a lot of energy is released. This energy can be harnessed to create electricity and other forms of energy. It can also be used in a powerful type of bomb known as the atomic bomb. This is the type of bomb that was dropped on the Japanese cities of Hiroshima and Nagasaki during World War II. When a nucleus of an atom is broken apart for any reason, it is known as nuclear fission. This is different from nuclear fusion, which is when two nuclei are combined.

where women, especially Jewish women, were not accepted. Today, she is still a role model and inspiration to women.

Words to Know

Potential: having the ability to become or do something in the future.
Element: one of the substances that make up everything in the world, and which cannot be broken down into simpler substances.
Resolve: firm decision; dedication.

Find Out More

Hamilton, Janet. *Lise Meitner: Pioneer of Nuclear Fission*. Berkeley Heights, New Jersey: Enslow, 2002.

Jewish Women's Archive, "Lise Meitner"
www.jwa.org/encyclopedia/article/meitner-lise

Sime, Ruth Lewin. *Lise Meitner: A Life in Physics*. Berkeley: University of California, 2006.

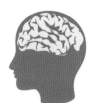

3

Katharine Blodgett:

Physicist & Inventor

S ome physicists use their knowledge to invent new things. In Katharine's case, she made many discoveries and turned them into something useful.

Katharine Blodgett was born on January 10, 1898, in New York State. Her father was killed before her birth, leaving Katharine's mother alone to raise her children. When Katharine was still a baby, her moved to Europe, and Katharine spent much of her early childhood there. When she returned to the United States as a teenager, she was enrolled in a private school in New York City. She excelled there, especially in mathematics. For her excellence in science, Katharine was rewarded a **scholarship** to Bryn Mawr College and chose to attend. While at Bryn Mawr College, Katharine studied mathematics and physics.

Before Katharine's father died, he had worked at General Electric (GE). After Katharine graduated from college in 1917, she tried to join GE too. She was not even twenty at the time. After touring the laboratory, she was told that she would need more education before she could be considered for the job. So Katharine chose to pursue a master's degree at the University of Chicago.

Her specific area of study involved gas masks. World War I was going on, and the gas mask was an important piece of technology to protect a soldier from poison gas. As young as she was, Katharine was already making discoveries. She found that one element, carbon, absorbed poison well, meaning it was a good addition to gas masks. She published these findings when she was only twenty-one years old.

After Katharine earned a master's degree, General Electric decided to hire her as a research scientist. At the time, she was the first and only female to work for the company. She sometimes worked with the same people who had worked with her father. At General Electric, Katharine worked with very thin coatings that could be placed on certain materials.

Earning a master's degree was not enough for Katharine. She wanted to earn a PhD, and she made history in the process. In 1926, she became the first female to graduate from Cambridge University with a doctorate in physics. At the same time, she was still working for General Electric.

What Is a Patent?

Like many inventors before her, Katharine came up with some unique ideas. She filed and received many patents in her lifetime. The government gives out patents. To receive one, you must apply for it. The papers for a patent contain important information such as what the patented invention is, when it was first created, and who owns it. Patents help protect an inventor from theft. This way, if someone tried to steal Katharine's ideas, she could prove that she had them first. Today, a lot of patent information can be viewed online.

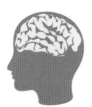

Katharine's work as a physicist allowed her to make many discoveries that involved applying very thin coatings to certain materials. One of her most famous was the invention of "invisible glass." Even though most light passes through glass, some of it is still reflected. That is why you can see glass when you look at it. The new coating Katharine invented bent the light that hit the glass so that it appeared more transparent, or invisible. Today, this coating is partially named after her. It is known as the Langmuir-Blodgett Film.

Katharine Blodgett died in 1979 at the age of eighty-one. She was given many awards in her lifetime, including being named as one of fifteen "Women of Achievement" by the U.S. Chamber of Commerce in 1951. Her hometown of Schenectady, New York, also named a day after her in 1951; June 13th is now celebrated as Katharine Blodgett Day. More recently, in 2008, an elementary school in Schenectady was named after her. Her influence extends far beyond her hometown, however. She was a courageous physicist who set herself high goals—and then achieved them.

Words to Know

Scholarship: money given to someone to attend college, based on their merits.

Find Out More

American Physical Society, "This Month in Physics History: March 16, 1938: Katharine Blodgett Patents Anti-Reflective Coatings"
www.aps.org/publications/apsnews/200703/history.cfm

Chemical Heritage Foundation, "Irving Langmuir and Katharine Burr Blodgett"
www.chemheritage.org/discover/online-resources/chemistry-in-history/themes/microelectronics-and-nanotechnology/langmuir-blodgett.aspx

LEMELSON-MIT, "Katharine J. Blodgett"
web.mit.edu/invent/iow/blodgett.html

4

Maria Goeppert-Mayer:
Nuclear Shells

While a physicist is conducting research, she might find that another scientist is interested in the same thing. This was the case with Maria Goeppert-Mayer. While she was working on the nuclear shell model, she discovered that some other scientists were as well. These scientists were halfway across the world, in Germany. Despite the distance, she chose to work with these scientists. Together, they made more progress than they might have made alone. Working as a team had its advantages!

Maria Goeppert-Mayer was born on June 28, 1906, in Prussia. As a young girl, she moved to Germany and began her education. Maria was very promising and bright. She chose to enroll at the University of Göttingen, where her father had worked. Some of her professors were very famous scientists. They included

Max Born, James Franck, and Adolf Otto Reinhold Windaus. All three of them received Nobel Prizes.

While still in Germany, Maria earned a PhD in physics. She also married a man by the name of Joseph Edward Mayer. The two then chose to move to the United States. Maria was recognized for her intelligence, but she was held back because she was female. It was very difficult for Maria to find a teaching job. She eventually began working at Sarah Lawrence University as an instructor. Maria also held a research position at Columbia University.

In order to be successful, all Maria needed was a chance to prove her worth. Finally, by doing well at Columbia University, she was able to become an associate professor of physics there. Maria also worked for the Argonne National Laboratory. She was a senior physicist working in the **theoretical physics** division. There she began to think about nuclear shells.

At the same time, some physicists in Germany were thinking about nuclear shells, too. The most well known of these is J. Hans D. Jensen. Maria chose to work with these scientists toward their common goal of strengthening the nuclear shell model. Because she spent time in Germany as a little girl, she was able to communicate with them. In 1963, Maria Goeppert-Mayer and J. Hans D. Jensen were awarded the Nobel Prize in Physics for their work on the nuclear shell model.

Nuclear Shells

Because atoms are tiny, no one can look inside them and see what is happening. Physicists must use math to figure out what could be going on at such small scale. Maria Goeppert-Mayer thought up a theory for how the parts of a nucleus move. She referred to these parts as being part of shells and believed that each "shell" moved in a certain way. This theory explained why some elements were stable while others were unstable.

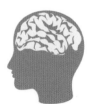

Maria Goeppert-Mayer died in 1972 at the age of sixty-five, but she is remembered as an inspiration. Many awards have been named in her honor. These awards are given to promising female scientists. The Maria Goeppert-Mayer Symposium is held once a year, a place for female researchers to come together and discuss new developments in science. A crater on Venus has also been named after her, as well as a unit in photon measurement.

The world has finally recognized Maria Goeppert-Mayer's intelligence and **ingenuity**!

Words to Know

Theoretical physics: the use of math and computers to make predictions about natural processes.
Ingenuity: cleverness, inventiveness.

Find Out More

Ferry, Joseph. *Maria Goeppert Mayer, Physicist*. Philadelphia, Penn.: Chelsea House, 2003.

Nobel Prize, "The Nobel Prize in Physics 1963: Eugene Wigner, Maria Goeppert Mayer, J. Hans D. Jensen: Biography"
www.nobelprize.org/nobel_prizes/physics/laureates/1963/mayer-bio.html

San Diego Supercomputer Center, "Maria Goeppert-Mayer"
www.sdsc.edu/ScienceWomen/mayer.html

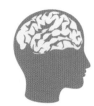

Chien-Shiung Wu: Understanding the Atom

5

Many physicists make important discoveries. Some affect the world more than others. In Chien-Shiung Wu's case, her research helped develop a new type of bomb. This bomb was a terrible thing, but it did change history.

Chien-Shiung Wu was born on May 31, 1912, in China. At the time, especially in China, women did not often receive the same education as men. Female scientists were not common. However, Chien-Shiung's family supported her desire to go to school. The first school she attended was one her parents had started themselves. After a few years, she went to another school that was specifically for women. Then in 1929, Chien-Shiung began attending National Central University.

Chien-Shiung's research at Columbia University involved shooting proton beams through pipes to confirm a type of subatomic behavior known as "weak interaction."

As part of her training, Chien-Shiung was required to teach for a short while. She continued learning and doing research until she graduated from college with a degree in physics. After college, she became a researcher of physics in China. There was a problem, though. Chien-Shiung knew her level of education limited

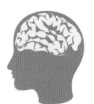

The Manhattan Project

Many anthropologists choose to become an expert in one area. In Margaret's case, she chose the South Pacific Islands. Choosing a specialization has a few advantages. First, it allows an anthropologist to learn a lot about one culture. Second, it allows anthropologists to compare two close cultures in order to find what makes them similar and what makes them different. Finally, it allows an anthropologist to stay in one place for a long time. By staying in one geographic location, an anthropologist can truly get to know what she is studying. She can interview the people of the area, examine the living conditions, and experience the climate.

her. She wanted to go to another country to continue studying. She applied and was accepted to the University of California at Berkeley. She left China to go to her new school in 1936. Moving across the world to obtain an education might seem difficult, but Chien-Shiung wasn't going to let anything stand in her way!

In Berkeley, Chien-Shiung studied with one of the most well-known physicists of the time, Ernest O. Lawrence. He received the Nobel Prize for Physics in 1939.

Chien-Shiung earned her PhD in 1940 and soon began teaching. She moved to the East Coast of the United States and spent time teaching at Smith College, Princeton University, and Columbia University.

At Columbia University, Chien-Shiung Wu took part in one of the most important projects of her day. It was known as the Manhattan Project, and the research done for the project eventually helped create the atomic bomb.

After World War II was over, Chien-Shiung Wu studied particle physics in other ways. Certain chemicals slowly decay. When this happens, they lose protons and become other elements. These elements are usually more stable. As this process happens, harmful energy is released. This dangerous energy is known as radiation. It cannot be seen, but radiation's effects can be felt. Radiation can hurt living things. Chien-Shiung researched how radiation can be measured and how it occurs.

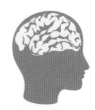

Chien-Shiung Wu (left) and her associates, Dr. Y.K. Lee and L.W. Mo (right), are shown conducting their experiments at Columbia University in 1963.

One of the discoveries she and her colleagues made changed what physicists thought about nature. Scientists had thought everything at an atomic level was done in a symmetrical or uniform way. She proved that this was not true.

Chien-Shiung continued teaching at Columbia University until she retired in 1980. She died on February 16, 1997, at the age of eighty-four.

Some of Chien-Shiung Wu's **colleagues** received the Nobel Prize for Physics, but she was not included. However, she did receive many other honors and is recognized today as the "First Lady of Physics."

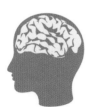

Words to Know

Colleagues: people one works with.

Find Out More

Columbia University, "Chien-Shiung Wu"
c250.columbia.edu/c250_celebrates/remarkable_columbians/chien-shiung_
wu.html

Cooperman, Stephanie. *Chien-Shiung Wu: Pioneering Physicist and Atomic Researcher*. New York: Rosen, 2004.

National Women's History Museum, "Dr. Chien-Shiung Wu (1912–1997)"
www.nwhm.org/education-resources/biography/biographies/chien-shiung-wu

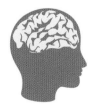

6

Ursula Franklin:
Physicist, Feminist, & Pacifist

Sometimes, being a scientist is not enough. To make a real difference, you must speak up. Ursula Franklin's knowledge in science helped her make a difference. She used a scientific approach to explain why violence is bad. According to her, nothing good would ever come from being violent. She also examined technology and how it influences society as a whole.

Ursula Franklin was born in 1921 in Germany. From a young age, she experienced **discrimination** and **prejudice**. As a child, she was forced to go to a Nazi work camp because of her Jewish heritage.

As Ursula grew older, she chose to study physics. In 1948, she graduated with a PhD from the Technical University of Berlin. A year later, Ursula moved to Canada and began working at the University of Toronto.

Ursula Franklin, Feminist

Feminists believe in and fight for equality between men and women. Like many female scientists, Ursula felt the pressures of being a minority in the scientific world. As an outspoken woman, Ursula was not shy about demanding better for women both inside and outside of the workplace. During Ursula's time as a professor at the University of Toronto, women were not paid the same salaries as men. Ursula and several other female professors eventually demanded better and won.

Ursula was a woman of many firsts. She became University of Toronto's first female professor in metallurgy and **materials science** in 1967. Metallurgy is the study of how metals interact with one another. Certain metals can be combined to create alloys. These alloys are usually lighter but stronger than pure metals. Different elements connect to each other and form bonds. Some compounds are stronger than others. If you combine a strong metal with a weak metal, it might become strong and bendable but also very light.

Some of Ursula's work was very important. She was researching radioactivity when nuclear weapons were being tested. The radioactivity of these bombs was harmful to humans. Over time, poisoning from radioactivity can slowly destroy your body. Ursula's findings helped control testing so that it did not hurt people in the process.

This was not the only way Ursula found to help people. She also cared about the environment and the resources it provides us. One of Ursula's greatest passions was trying to protect all living things.

Through her research, Ursula found that a lot of money being used by the government was going toward the military. She wanted to change this. Ursula believed in peace instead of war. She was a pacifist, a person who believes in non-violence. As a member of the Canadian Voice of Women for Peace, she pushed for research to be done on protecting the environment rather than developing weapons.

Ursula's beliefs about physics and pacifism eventually came together. She combined the two in her opinions about technology. According to her, technology influences society. Whether it has a good effect or a bad effect is up to the people that make and use it. Much of technology today is produced in factories. The people making the piece of technology are very disconnected from it. Usually, they are told what to do and have no control over it. Ursula believes that when a creator is allowed to finish his own work, from start to finish, it will be better.

Ursula has spent over forty years at the University of Toronto. In 1984, she was named a University Professor at the University of Toronto. At the time, she was the first and only woman to be given this title, the highest rank a professor can earn. Recently, in 2012, she was **inducted** into the Canadian Science and Engineering Hall of Fame. A high school is named after her as well, the Ursula Franklin Academy in Toronto. Ursula remains an active part of the school, influencing another generation of scientists.

Words to Know

Discrimination: denying a person an opportunity based on that person's ethnicity, sexual orientation, religion, or other identifying factor.
Prejudice: the belief that people of certain social groups are inferior.
Materials science: the study of the structure and properties of what things are made out of.
Inducted: elected into.

Find Out More

Canada Science and Technology Museum, "Ursula Martius Franklin"
www.sciencetech.technomuses.ca/english/about/hallfame/u_i53_e.cfm

Franklin, Ursula M. *The Ursula Franklin Reader: Pacifism as a Map*. Toronto, Ont.: Between the Lines, 2006.

The United Nations Association in Canada, "Pearson Peace Medal > Dr. Ursula M Franklin, O.C. FRSC (2001)"
www.unac.org/en/news_events/pearson/2001.asp

7

Argelia Velez-Rodriguez:
Physicist & Minority Educator

Not all female scientists have the same opportunities growing up. When Argelia Velez-Rodriguez lived in Cuba, she was accepted as a woman who wanted to learn about math and science. She did not face the difficulties female scientists in the United States faced at the time. Then when she moved to the United States, she became a teacher. After arriving in America, she noticed that not everyone had an equal opportunity to do well. Argelia wanted to change this.

Argelia was born in 1936 in Cuba. She was very good at mathematics as a young girl. She even won a medal for her skills in arithmetic when she was only nine years old. Then, as an adult, Argelia began studying mathematics at the Marianao Institute. She earned a bachelor's degree from this school in 1955.

Women who wanted to study science in Cuba were encouraged. In fact, the university she chose to go to had mostly women instructors. Many of them had **doctorates**. However, Argelia was black. Not a single black woman had received a doctorate in mathematics before Argelia came along. But Argelia changed that!

Argelia's interest in math led naturally to an interest in physics as well. The two fields of study intersect in many ways, including math formulas that describe the movement of planets and other objects in space. This was one of Argelia's interests.

Argelia received a doctorate in mathematics from the University of Havana in 1960. By this time, she also had two children, and she wanted them to receive a proper education as well. This was a dream that came true: her son would one day become a surgeon, while her daughter would become an engineer.

About the time that Argelia earned her PhD, Fidel Castro came to power as the leader of Cuba's government. Not everyone supported Castro, and conflicts and civil unrest were common. Argelia did not feel safe having her children there, so she decided to move to the United States.

As a black female scientist in America, Argelia faced discrimination. Even though she was well educated and had the PhD to prove it, people treated her differently. This was very different from her life in Cuba, where she had been respected.

Argelia got a job teaching at the University of Texas in 1962. Later she also taught at Bishop College. She taught classes in mathematics and physics.

In 1970, she became still more deeply involved in education. Because of her own experiences, Argelia understood how hard it was for **minorities** to receive a proper education in the United States. She thought up ways that might help them and other disadvantaged students succeed.

In 1972, Argelia became an American citizen. Soon after this, she joined the U.S. Department of Education, where she became the director of the Minority

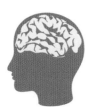

Science Improvement Program. This program helps minority students excel in the sciences. Argelia is working hard to help minorities pursue careers in math and science!

Words to Know

Doctorates: advanced educational degrees also known as PhDs.
Minorities: people who are different from the rest of the group they belong to.

Find Out More

Agnes Scott College, "Argelia Velez-Rodriguez"
www.agnesscott.edu/lriddle/women/rodrig.htm

Buffalo College, "Black Women in Mathematics: Argelia Velez-Rodriguez"
www.math.buffalo.edu/mad/PEEPS/velez-rodriguez_argelia.html

University of St Andrews, Scotland, "Argelia Velez-Rodriguez"
www-history.mcs.st-and.ac.uk/Biographies/Velez-Rodriguez.html

U.S. Department of Education,
"Minority Science and Engineering Improvement Program"
www2.ed.gov/programs/iduesmsi/index.html

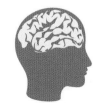

8

Sau Lan Wu
Accelerating Particles

Sometimes physicists come up with **theories** that cannot be proven in their lifetimes. Other scientists will then try to prove these theories right or wrong. The standard model of particles is one such theory. It was developed early in the twentieth century. Sau Lan Wu is one of the physicists who are working on proving it. Today, we are very close to proving that it is fact.

Sau Lan Wu was born in Hong Kong, China. She originally wanted to be a painter—but then she read a biography of Marie Curie, a famous female scientist. Marie Curie studied radioactivity and how it affects living things. She was the first woman to win a Nobel Prize. Sau Lan Wu was inspired by her story. She decided she wanted to be a physicist.

Getting the right education, however, was difficult for Sau Lan Wu. Her parents would not pay for her to go to college. Sau Lan Wu would not give up, though. She looked through many books to find a college that seemed right for her, and then she applied to several colleges in the United States. If she could obtain a scholarship, she knew she could attend a school for free.

Sau Lan Wu got a scholarship to Vassar College. When she came to the United States, she did not speak English very well. Being in a foreign country was difficult for her, but the people at Vassar were helpful. Determined to be a great physicist, Sau Lan Wu studied very hard.

She graduated in 1963. She had done so well that now she could take her pick from the best graduate schools, including Yale, Harvard, Berkeley, Columbia, and Massachusetts Institute of Technology (MIT). She received a master's degree from Harvard University in 1964. Four years later, she completed her doctorate. Her dream had come true. She had become a physicist.

Since then, Sau Lan Wu has been a part of several teams that have discovered something new in the world of physics. While doing research at MIT, she helped find a new particle. This particle was even smaller than protons, electrons, and

The Higgs Boson Particle

Some particle physicists have theorized that one particle is the reason why objects have mass. On Earth, mass is the same as weight. In 2012, Sau Lan Wu and some fellow scientists made an important discovery that supported the existence of the Higgs particle, or Higgs Boson. This particle is what physicists believe gives objects mass. Scientists are still not entirely positive the particle exists, but there is a lot of evidence that supports its existence. This particle would explain why the universe is the way it is. It is the last particle that needs to be discovered before the standard model of particles is accepted.

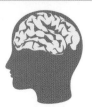

The tunnel of the Large Hadron Collider in Switzerland, where atoms are smashed against each other at very high speeds.

Particle Accelerators

Sau Lan Wu often travels to Switzerland so that she can use the Large Hadron Collider to conduct her research. This is one of the most powerful particle accelerators in the world. To separate subatomic particles from an atom, they must be split apart by force. One way is with a particle accelerator. It's a scientific instrument that makes charged particles such as protons and electrons go very fast. This acceleration is achieved by using focused magnetic fields to route the beam of particles through a sealed vacuum chamber. The nucleus of one atom smashes into another atom, breaking it apart. This reaction releases a lot of energy. It also changes the atoms in the process.

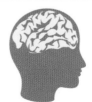

San Lau uses enormous machines like this one to investigate the Higgs boson, the thing that joins our world together and gives it matter.

neutrons. The existence of these particles proves that atoms are not the smallest unit, and there is something even smaller.

Most of her work from then on looked at these tiny particles, known as elementary particles. Today, elementary particles are considered the smallest possible pieces of matter. Physicists think there are seventeen types of elementary particles in total. Sau Lan Wu has helped to discover two of them.

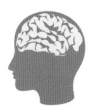

In between her research, Sau Lan Wu teaches others. She is currently a professor at the University of Wisconsin. Explaining her discoveries to others is one of her passions.

Sau Lan Wu has received plenty of recognition for her research. She is the first American to be awarded the European Physical Society High-Energy and Particle Physics Prize. Sau Lan Wu is also a fellow of the American Academy of Arts and Sciences. Her example proves what hard work and determination combined with intelligence can achieve.

Words to Know

Theories: explanations based on good scientific evidence.

Find Out More

University of Wisconsin, "Professor Sau Lan Wu"
www-wisconsin.cern.ch/~wus/

Vassar Alumnae, "Sau Lan Wu '63 Discusses God Particle Discovery"
alums.vassar.edu/news/2012-2013/121107-sau-lan-wu.html

Vassar College, "Going after the God Particle"
innovators.vassar.edu/innovator.html?id=72

9

Shirley Ann Jackson:
Presidential Advisor

S hirley Ann Jackson is a role model for both women and black Americans. She helped prove to the world that an African American woman can be an amazing physicist.

Shirley was born on August 5, 1946, in Washington, D.C. As a young girl, she became interested in mathematics and science. She loved to explore the natural world. Shirley's father helped her do her science projects when she was a child, encouraging her interest in both her schoolwork and the world around her. Above all else, Shirley wanted to know how things worked and why. This drive caused her to do very well in school.

Shirley says her advice to young people is: "Aim for the stars, so that at least you can reach the treetops."

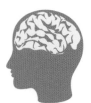 48　WOMEN IN PHYSICS

When Shirley graduated from high school, she was the valedictorian; she had gotten better grades than anyone else in her whole class. There was never a question about whether or not she would go to college!

As a promising student, Shirley had a lot of schools to choose from. Harvard University, the University of Chicago, and Brown University all accepted her, but Shirley decide to attend the Massachusetts Institute of Technology (MIT).

When she first began college in 1964, black students were not common on the MIT campus. In fact, Shirley was the only African American who was studying her major—theoretical physics—at MIT that year.

After graduating in 1968, Shirley began working toward her PhD. She stayed at MIT to do this and majored in particle physics, studying the subatomic particles that make up the world around us. Shirley made history once again in 1973 when she became the first African American woman to earn a PhD from MIT.

After earning her doctorate, her first few jobs were in business laboratories where she did research. Research physicists spend their time conducting experiments. These experiments help us expand our knowledge of physics. Many of Shirley's jobs required that she apply her understanding of theoretical physics to the real world. After many years of hard work, Shirley was now considered an expert in her field.

Some of Shirley's time was also spent teaching others and conducting research at universities. This gave her the experience she needed to climb even higher. Shirley eventually gained recognition on a national scale. In 1995, former President Clinton asked her to join the United States Nuclear Regulatory Commission (NRC) as the chairperson. The NRC makes sure that we are handling nuclear energy in a responsible way. Shirley was the first woman and first African American to hold this position.

In 1999, Shirley Ann Jackson achieved another significant accomplishment. She was elected as the eighteenth president of Rensselaer Polytechnic Institute, the first woman and first African American to hold that position.

Shirley has been honored in other ways as well. She was inducted into the National Women's Hall of Fame in 1998. Then, in 2009, a president of the United States once again called upon Shirley. This time, President Obama asked her

to be part of the President's Council of Advisors on Science and Technology (PCAST). This council helps the government make decisions that involve science.

Shirley Ann Jackson is truly an inspiration to all black Americans and all women. She proves that with enough effort and skill, any door can be opened!

Find Out More

My Growth Plan, "Dr. Shirley Ann Jackson"
www.mygrowthplan.org/Biographies/ShirleyAnnJackson.htm

O'Connell, Diane. *Strong Force: The Story of Physicist Shirley Ann Jackson*. New York: Franklin Watts, 2005.

Rensselaer Polytechnic Institute, "Shirley Ann Jackson, PhD"
www.rpi.edu/president/profile.html

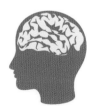

10

Lisa Randall: Unraveling the Universe's Mysteries

Where did the universe come from—and where is it going? Throughout history, many people have tried to find the answer to these questions. Ancient astronomers and philosophers came up with different theories. Today, some of those theories have been proven wrong while others are still possible. People like Lisa Randall spend their time researching these questions.

Lisa Randall was born on June 18, 1962, in New York City. She was always interested in physics and mathematics. When she was only eighteen, she won first place in the Westinghouse Science Talent Search. Lisa graduated from Harvard University just three years later, and then she went on to get her master's and doctor's degrees.

At Harvard, she studied both physics and cosmology. (Cosmologists try to figure out how the universe was formed and why. They might also look at why something like the universe is possible.) One of Lisa's possible explanations involves the existence of extra dimensions. She believes that these dimensions are warped and very different from our own.

In 1987, Lisa left Harvard with a PhD in particle physics. She then spent time researching and teaching at several universities, including Massachusetts Institute of Technology (MIT) and Princeton University. She returned to Harvard in 2001 as a professor and has been teaching there ever since. She also conducts research. Scientists are always eager to learn more!

In addition to her own studies, Lisa Randall is always looking for ways to get others interested. Physics is a science that has to do with all of us, but sometimes it can be confusing for others to grasp. Scientific papers are hard to read. Lisa Randall began publishing books about physics and cosmology that were intended to help ordinary people understand the latest developments in science. Some of the theories she presents are complex, but she does her best to explain them in a simple way.

Lisa's work has gained her a lot of recognition. In 2007, she was included in *Time Magazine*'s "100 Most Influential People." She was also one of forty people featured in the *Rolling Stone*'s 40th Anniversary Issue. Lisa has been on television and the radio, giving interviews and lectures. Her influence is so great that she is currently one of the most cited physicists of her time. This means that a lot of other physicists refer to her work in their own writing. As a female scientist, she proves to the entire world what a woman can do!

String Theory

One theory that Lisa Randall tries to explain is known as string theory. Physicists who believe in this theory consider the universe to be made up of fibers that are strung together. This theory helps make sense out of the way the universe behaves. String theory is part of theoretical physics because it has not yet been proven. However, it has not yet been disproven either!

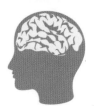

Extra Dimensions

Some physicists believe in extra dimensions. This can seem like something right out of a science fiction novel! However, physicists have found reasons to suggest that our dimension is not the only one.

Currently, we are aware of three directions. Think about the way you move in the world. You can go left and right, forward and backward, and up and down. This is how most objects are measured. This book is three-dimensional because you can measure its length, width, and height.

Some physicists believe that there might be more directions than the three we can see and feel. Lisa Randall is one of those scientists.

Find Out More

Randall, Lisa. *Knocking on Heaven's Door: How Physics and Scientific Thinking Illuminate the Universe and the Modern World*. New York: Ecco, 2012.

Randall, Lisa. *Warped Passages: Unraveling the Mysteries of the Universe's Hidden Dimensions*. New York: Harper Perennial, 2006.

Harvard University, "Faculty: Lisa Randall"
www.physics.harvard.edu/people/facpages/randall.html

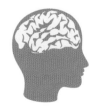

11

Opportunities for Women in Physics Today

Physicists are in high demand in the twenty-first century. They can earn around $100,000 a year, and this salary might increase for a more experienced physicist.

If you decide you want to be a physicist, your three main options for a job are: teaching at a university, working for the government, and working for a company. What your role will be in each of these situations will vary by what you know.

That's because there are many different types of physicists. Particle physicists deal with atoms and what they are made out of. Astrophysicists look at how

Betsy Pugel is a physicist who works for NASA—but that doesn't mean she's out in space! Here she's helping to educate kids by showing students an imprint of a boot from a space suit.

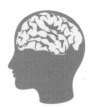

Priyamvada Nataraja is an astrophysicist at Yale University who helped discover enormous black holes, using the deepest X-ray image ever taken.

the objects in outer space move. Theoretical physicists use math to solve problems based on something we cannot prove yet. These are only three of the many different areas of physics in which a person can specialize. Some physicists work in all three areas at one time or another.

Working for the Government

About a quarter of physicists in the United States work for the government. These physicists often help to keep our country safe. They may work on new weapons, or they may protect U.S. soldiers by creating better equipment.

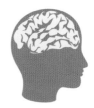

Not all physicists who work for the government focus on war, however. Some work on projects that can help our nation in a peaceful way. This includes research into energy and how it is harnessed. Nuclear energy is very powerful but can also be dangerous. If not handled properly, it can cause terrible harm to human life. Particle physicists understand this energy better than anyone else, so they are the ones who continue to improve on it.

Physicists are also a very big part of NASA's team. Some of the best physicists have helped design vehicles that can be used in space. They research how a spacecraft is affected by leaving and entering Earth's atmosphere. Physicists may also help analyze the discoveries made by researchers who have gone into space.

Working for a Company

Sometimes, a company with a lot of money might want to invest in a certain area of research. A physicist will then be paid to perform this research. Anything discovered by a research physicist can be used to make products for that company.

There are many benefits—including including higher salaries and potential ownership of company stock—that come with working for a company. However, as an employee, you are required to do what a company tells you. There often isn't as much freedom within a company, but the pay can be very good. About a quarter of all physicists in the United States work for a company or scientific firm.

Teaching

Many physicists work at a university. They teach or **mentor** students. They conduct research that is funded by the university. Often, students are asked to help with this research.

Performing research at a university might give a physicist more freedom than working with the government or a company. Often physicists apply for **grants** to conduct their research. Anything they discover will be credited to them and the school that helped fund their research.

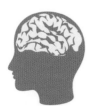

Sometimes physicists DO end up in space! On June 18, 1983, a young physicist from California took her seat aboard the space shuttle and launched into history. On that date, Sally Ride became the first American woman in space as a mission specialist.

Pay

The median annual wage of physicists was $106,370 in 2010. (The median wage is the wage at which half the workers in an occupation earned more than that amount and half earned less.) The lowest 10 percent earned less than $58,850, and the top 10 percent earned at least $166,400.

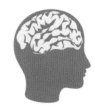

Sometimes physicists work to solve health problems. Here health physicist techni-
cians from the U.S. Army and the Department of Energy take environmental samples
that could have dangerous nuclear radiation.

On average, physicists who work for the government make the most money.
Their median wages are $137,420. Physicists who do research and development
for private businesses have a median wage of $92,040, while those who work for
universities and colleges have a median wage of $64,070.

Job Outlook

Employment of physicists is expected to increase by 14 percent from 2010 to
2020, as fast as the average for all other occupations.

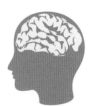

The government is the main source of physics-related research funds, especially for basic research. Additional government funding for energy and for manufacturing research is expected to increase the overall need for physicists.

Declines in basic research are expected to be offset by growth in **applied research** in private industry. People with a physics background will continue to be in demand in medicine, **information technology**, **communications technology**, **semiconductor technology**, and other applied **research-and-development** fields.

The **competition** for permanent research appointments, such as those at colleges and universities, is expected to be strong. More and more, even if you have a PhD, you'll need to work through several jobs before finding a permanent position. In addition, the number of research proposals submitted for funding has been growing faster than the amount of funds available, causing more competition for research grants.

Despite the competition for research jobs, prospects should be good for physicists in applied research, development, and related technical fields. Graduates with any academic degree in physics or astronomy, from bachelor's degree to doctorate, will find their knowledge of science and mathematics useful for entry into many other occupations.

All this is true for both male and female physicists in the years to come. Thanks to the courageous and gifted women physicists of both today and the past, women will have many opportunities in this field in the years to come.

Words to Know

Mentor: a person who advises and guides a less-experienced person.

Grants: money given to a person or organization for a particular reason, often for research.

Applied research: investigations directed toward a specific purpose or goal, such as developing a new product.

Information technology: the use of computers to store and communicate data and ideas.

Communications technology: the equipment and programs used to transfer information from one place to another.

Semiconductor technology: the use and study of materials that can transmit electricity.

Research-and-development: work directed toward the creation of and improvement of products and processes.

Competition: the fight to win.

Find Out More

Bureau of Labor Statistics, "Physicist"
www.bls.gov/k12/math04.htm#jobs

Institute for Career Research. *Career as a Physicist: Studying How the Universe Works and Using Your Knowledge to Play an Integral Part in Future Advances in Medicine, Computers, National Defense, Lasers, Transportation, Energy Efficiency and the Environment.* Chicago: Institute for Career Research, 2003.

Physics.org, "Careers from Physics"
www.physics.org/careers.asp?contentid=381

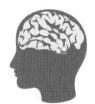

Index

About the Author & Consultant

Shaina Indovino is a writer and illustrator living in Nesconset, New York. She graduated from Binghamton University, where she received degrees in Sociology and English. She enjoyed the opportunity to apply both her areas of study to a topic that excites her: women in science. She hopes more young women will follow their calling toward what they truly love, whether it be science related or not.

Ann Lee-Karlon, PhD, is the President of the Association for Women in Science (AWIS) in 2014–2016. AWIS is a national nonprofit organization dedicated to advancing women in science, technology, engineering, and mathematics. Dr. Lee-Karlon also serves as Senior Vice President at Genentech, a major biotechnology company focused on discovering and developing medicines for serious diseases such as cancer. Dr. Lee-Karlon holds a BS in Bioengineering from the University of California at Berkeley, an MBA from Stanford University, and a PhD in Bioengineering from the University of California at San Diego, where she was a National Science Foundation Graduate Research Fellow. She completed a postdoctoral fellowship at the University College London as an NSF International Research Fellow. Dr. Lee-Karlon holds several U.S. and international patents in vascular and tissue engineering.

Picture Credits

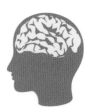